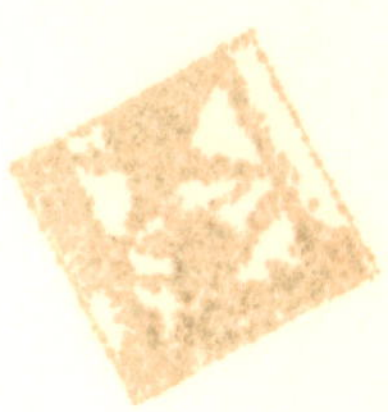

Ecology

Ecology

◄— A FIRST BOOK —►

Man's Effects on his Environment and its Mechanisms

by JOHN HOKE

Illustrated by
RICHARD CUFFARI

Franklin Watts, Inc.
845 Third Avenue
New York, New York 10022

SBN 531-00745-6
Copyright © 1971 by Franklin Watts, Inc.
Library of Congress Catalog Card Number: 74-153860
Printed in the United States of America
5 6 7 8 9 10

Introduction

No other creature on earth has changed the earth's environment in so many gross ways as has man. This book deals with the way man has brought these changes about.

The study of our earth's environment — ecology — has become so vast that it overlaps and includes a number of other scientific areas. It is outlined here in only that detail necessary to present its whole image, to suggest the scope of its vast coverage — and to provide an adequate framework in which to view man's past works. With this background we can judge whether past actions were wise or unwise, and we can plan the best ways man can deal with the environment in the future.

Part One

Ecology–The Study of the Home

The Home Man Has Made

About three-quarters of all Americans live today in a city or suburban environment, in surroundings created by man. Of all earth's creatures, only man has developed an extensive ability to shape and change the environment to suit his wants and needs. And he is doing this in many ways: Better roadways and sidewalks are being made from concrete and asphalt than from packed dirt. Homes and other buildings are being constructed in which we can escape the effects of outside weather we do not like. Technology has produced a host of products to enrich our lives — such as radio, television, and hi-fi music systems, able to bring us scenes and sounds from far away and out of the past. The automobile and airplane have extended man's physical reach to the point that a trip around the world is no longer the unique adventure it was years ago. Automatic kitchens and other new equipment and materials go further to make our lives more comfortable. This period of man's time on earth might best be described as the Modern Industrial Society.

What has the nature of modern life to do with ecology? A great deal. The word "ecology" comes from two Greek words that mean "the study of the home." As a scientific name it describes the study of the ways in which all the life-forms on earth relate and interrelate with each other, and how they exist in and respond to their physical environment. "Environment" is a word with broad meaning, for any location can under certain circumstances be considered an environment. But the word can also refer to a type of area, such as a desert environment, a woodland environment, or an urban environment. The particular place we live in can be described as our home environment.

In recent years the words "ecology" and "environment" have become increasingly important, for what man has done to shape a special environment for himself has had a more and more pronounced effect on the general environment of the world. And not by any means have all of these man-caused changes been good.

These changes show up in many different ways — both great and small. By building big cities, the immediate climate can be changed. Asphalt streets and buildings of stone and glass create canyons where summer temperatures can grow unbearably hot. In the winter, outdoor temperatures in a city are often a number of degrees higher than in the more open suburbs and countryside surrounding the city. A snowfall that covers the ground for days in the countryside may soon

be slush in a nearby city, or even fall as rain. Automobile exhaust and furnace smoke in the city can make the air unpleasant to breathe. Even worse fumes come from city incinerators burning trash.

In many cases, the changes man has made in his environment have become a permanent part of his living situation. With the passing years, more and more such basic changes are affecting the whole environment — and the ecological processes that shape it and take place *in* it.

Ecology — The Most Broad-Based Life Science

Ecology, as a science and area for study, includes and touches upon many other sciences. Biology, geology, and climatology are but a few of the specific areas of science that are involved and are a vital part of the field of ecology. While accomplished scientists in the fields of biology have a working understanding of ecological principles, they tend to concentrate on their main area of study and training. For this reason, ecology has recently become a specialized branch of science. With increasing concern being raised over the condition of our environment, more and more attention is now being given to finding scientific approaches able to deal in complete ways with the processes that change the environment and the mechanisms by which the environment and the life-forms that live in it are governed.

The "study of the home" suggests the completeness of the approach taken by ecologists: All the living beings and the physical setting that make up a "home" are related in some manner and affect each other. In the typical home we live in, for example, each family member has his place and is taken care of by the other family members. In the healthy home, there is an average climate in which all members can live. The home is kept clean; there is a nursery to care for the young. All members of the family are protected and fed. Individuals may exert themselves, but they are kept reasonably in check by other members. Death and other events bring changes, but these are counteracted by the birth of new life and other adjustments — so the "home" continues.

Although the term "ecology" may be new to many of us, ecological understanding goes far back in time. Long ago, primitive man foraged to feed and clothe himself, relying totally upon natural providence for his needs. But he soon learned enough about his environment to be able to know the best times and places to look for the things he needed. When he first began successfully to grow plants and to tend domesticated beasts, he was exploiting his understanding of ecological principles.

Throughout time, man learned increasingly more about the mechanisms of the environment, and in time increased his husbanding skills to where, today, one farmer is able to provide the food needs of great numbers of people. And those

farmers who accomplish this, without damaging the land and its environment, can be considered to be accomplished as ecologists. They may not know the terminology of the science — as they are practicing it — nor all facets of it, but their farming accomplishments show that they have a fair grasp of many of the intricate environmental mechanisms with which they are dealing.

A Dynamic Science

Ecology is a science that deals with materials in a constant state of change. There is very little about the environment that is static. Even where such absolutes as temperature ranges for a given life-form are concerned, there is variation — for should you try to fix some upper and lower limits, a few individuals of the affected life-form may actually endure beyond such limits, and as time passes, the species as a whole can adapt to endure the new extreme.

Ecology — Its Organization and Systems

There are two basic aspects to the science of ecology. They deal with the relationships between the living organisms on earth — called *life-forms* — and the relationships of the life-forms with the surrounding physical environment.

The physical nature of the environment strongly influences the life-forms that inhabit it. These *physical factors* include earth or soil and its chemical makeup, land elevation and topography, and temperature conditions. Water's various forms — moisture, humidity (the amount of water vapor in the atmosphere), rainfall, water drainage from the land, the mineral content of the water — are important factors. Air movement over the land is yet another important physical consideration, for it is the winds that transport life-supporting water vapor.

Living Organisms

In ecology each species of life is treated as a life-form, and ecologists focus their interest mainly upon how life-forms affect and interact with each other and the physical factors in their immediate environment. Where biologists may study an

individual animal, ecologists give equal attention to how the animal fits into its particular place in the environment, how the surroundings affect it, and how it in turn affects everything around it. Ecologists note such matters as the changes in the numbers of a given species in a particular area, how many young there are as compared to adults of the species, their reproduction rate, and male versus female ratios.

Equally important is the interrelationship that exists between the animals in a locality and the plant life that also lives there, and the physical factors that have a direct bearing on their lives.

Interaction of Life-Forms with Their Environment

Both the life-forms themselves and the physical factors in the environment determine what species of life can live in a particular place. Many physical factor variations, such as temperature and humidity, are not overly important to the life-forms in a given environment, just so long as the variations of these physical factors stay within limits. Where there is an abundance of a basic physical requirement — such as enough rainfall to create a humid atmosphere and plenty of soil moisture — it plays no limiting role on the life-forms it influences. But where this same physical factor *is* limited, it may prevent affected life-forms from existing in great numbers or keep them out of an environment altogether. The simple matter of space limits the numbers of a given species that can live in one locality.

In the sea, for example, open waters will be rich in oxygen — and can thus support large hosts of life-forms. But this same water trapped in shallow and warm tide pools may lose its rich oxygen content and no longer be able to support large numbers of the same life as it did earlier. Only those life-forms that are not affected by a lowered oxygen condition will be able to live in the water when it is trapped in a tidal pool.

A species of life exists only in a region where there is a proper amount of each single physical factor that is vital to its needs. For example, the geographic range of a given species ends where any one environmental condition has changed beyond the limit that species can endure. Such an environmental condition becomes one of that life-form's *limiting factors* — and it is these factors which set the boundary for all the members of that species.

The Physical Environment — A Series of Homes

The earth's environment is not a continuous one — in terms of a range from hot to cold, or wet to dry. Rather it is a series of "islands" wherein a particular set of conditions vital to one or a group of life-forms is able to meet all their life support needs. The temperature range is in keeping with their physical endurance. Water is available to them in the form they require — high or low humidity, ground moisture, standing water. There is adequate sunlight (or shade as the case may be). The boundaries of this "island" are located where any one of the set of physical conditions tapers off — or becomes excessive — so that the needs of this community of life cannot be met. Such an environment, its "package" of physical conditions (factors), and life-forms that inhabit it, is known as an *ecosystem*. The life-forms that inhabit an ecosystem are called its *biome*.

How the "Home" Is Structured

Scientists like to create a sense of order among the things they study, and ecologists are no different — they look at the world and its life as a series of organized units. As always in classifying a subject, they start with the whole and then identify and relate its parts.

In ecology, the "whole" is of course the whole world. Within the earth's thin blanket of air and water, all living things call someplace "home." In reality, this life-supporting blanket and its life is an ecosystem.

A scientist of the late nineteenth century, Alfred Wallace, divided the living matter of the world's continents into six areas known as zoogeographic realms. He established boundaries based upon bodies of water, high mountain ranges, and climatic factors, showing that physical conditions on either side of the boundary were markedly different. In each of these realms there were life-forms that did not exist in any of the other realms.

Scientists have also classified the land areas of the world in terms of what kinds of life are found in various places. In this overall view, the earth is best considered as an "ecosphere" with its giant biome that is the living part of the system. The life found on the earth's landmasses has been classified as falling into eight categories based upon the environmental conditions resulting from the interworking of the life-forms and physical factors of each location.

DECIDUOUS FOREST
CONIFEROUS FOREST
TUNDRA
GRASSLANDS
DESERT
TROPICAL FOREST
WOODLAND AND CHAPARRAL
SAVANNA

BIOMES OF THE EARTH

Characteristic vegetation forms are used to identify the eight categories of environmental conditions and the resulting life-forms that make up the land area of the earth. The life-form areas, or biomes, run latitudinally across the earth, parallel to the equator, since climate is the determining factor of the environments.

Each of the eight categories, called biomes, exhibits similar life-forms, regardless of where it may appear on earth. Physical conditions such as climate and season length are similar. Inasmuch as plant life plays a vital role in creating the conditions that determine what animal life can exist in each biome, there is a marked tendency for the plant and animal life-forms to be common to a given biome. Since plant life plays this important role, some of the biomes are named after the main or dominant vegetation found in the particular biome.

And so, beginning from the "whole" — the earth as a giant ecosystem or ecosphere — scientists have initially broken it up into six geographic regions (zoogeographic realms) and into eight groups of ecosystem life-forms, called biomes. From here, classification of the environment with its organized collections of physical factors and life-forms is treated as ecosystems within ecosystems. And these become smaller and smaller, to where an ecosystem can consist of the physical factors and life found in a rotten log, under a rock, or in a drop of water. One small ecosystem features a tiny wasp so small it must be viewed under a low-power microscope. It spends most of its life *inside* a tiny seed.

On land, while sets of related physical factors and life-forms — ecosystems — are treated in such terms as marsh or wetland ecosystems, forest ecosystems — desert or grasslands — these "divisions" are not absolute, for the natural environment does not lend itself to such arbitrary "fenced in" classification. There are many forms of life, particularly the more mobile animal forms, which may bridge one or another adjacent ecosystems that totally confine many life-forms. And so these individuals may roam the biomes of several side-by-side ecosystems — among life-forms in each biome that are themselves limited to just one particular ecosystem. So, rather than rigid borders, there is some blending. But for the main bulk of life in a given ecosystem, it is a "home" beyond whose boundaries life-forms do not wander. And scientists look to these more restricted life-forms to determine where one major ecosystem ends and another begins.

Life in an Ecosystem

The life-forms in an ecosystem — the biome — are in a constant dynamic state of change and adjustment. An ecosystem can be simple or complex and populated with but a few life-forms, or countless species of life. And the numbers of any given species are constantly shifting, as they are preyed upon or, in turn, consume some other forms of life. Such shifts and balances take place all the time and are tolerated normally without causing major upsets in the balance within the over-all ecosystem.

In the ecologist's view, an ecosystem is a single whole unit, made up of a system of well-organized parts and divided into living and nonliving matter. The physical factors set the stage in an ecosystem for the life that will live in it, although the life-forms themselves are also limiting factors. Topography and temperature are physical factors, as are the inorganic materials of the system. These include water and chemicals such as phosphorus, nitrogen, and carbon dioxide. And the form in which these materials exist plays an important role. It may be that the plant life in the system must process materials into forms that can be consumed by the animal life.

The life-forms of an ecosystem are divided into three types by ecologists: *producers*, *consumers*, and *decomposers*. All, in one way or another, are part of the food chain process of energy consumption in an ecosystem.

The Food Chains

Within each ecosystem most life-forms derive food energy from another life-form. However, the process begins with green plant life that produces its energy by converting sunlight into the plant material other life-forms consume. These first converters of solar energy into food substances that other life-forms can consume are known as *producers*. The life-forms that consume this plant life are called *consumers*. Those that consume only this green plant life are called *herbivores* — and in the food chain they are known as the *primary consumers.* Following next are the *predators* that consume the herbivores. Some predators also consume plant life, but since the predators consume the primary consumers, they are known as *secondary consumers.*

The third and final types of life-forms are the *decomposers.* They are the organisms that, by consuming dead organic matter, break it down into the materials and chemicals that can then be reused in the ecosystem to form new life. In the main, it is the producer life-forms that reuse these materials — and start them back through the vital food chain that supports life in the system.

Within a given food chain, all life-forms are ranked in some manner — in terms of what they consume, and how far up the line their consumption takes place. As an example, we can start with grass in one food chain. Most of us are familiar with this food chain because we are a part of it.

The grass grows by solar radiation, converting carbon dioxide gas in the atmosphere, and water, into plant food. Chlorophyll in the grass and chemicals in the soil play a vital role in this process, known as photosynthesis.

The grass is in turn consumed by a number of primary consumers — herbivores — such as beef and milk-producing cattle, or sheep and goats.

The herbivores are in turn preyed upon by a number of *carnivores* — meat-eating animals — which are the first predators and secondary consumers in the food chain.

Man is a secondary consumer and is among the predators that consume some of the herbivores. We eat the meat and

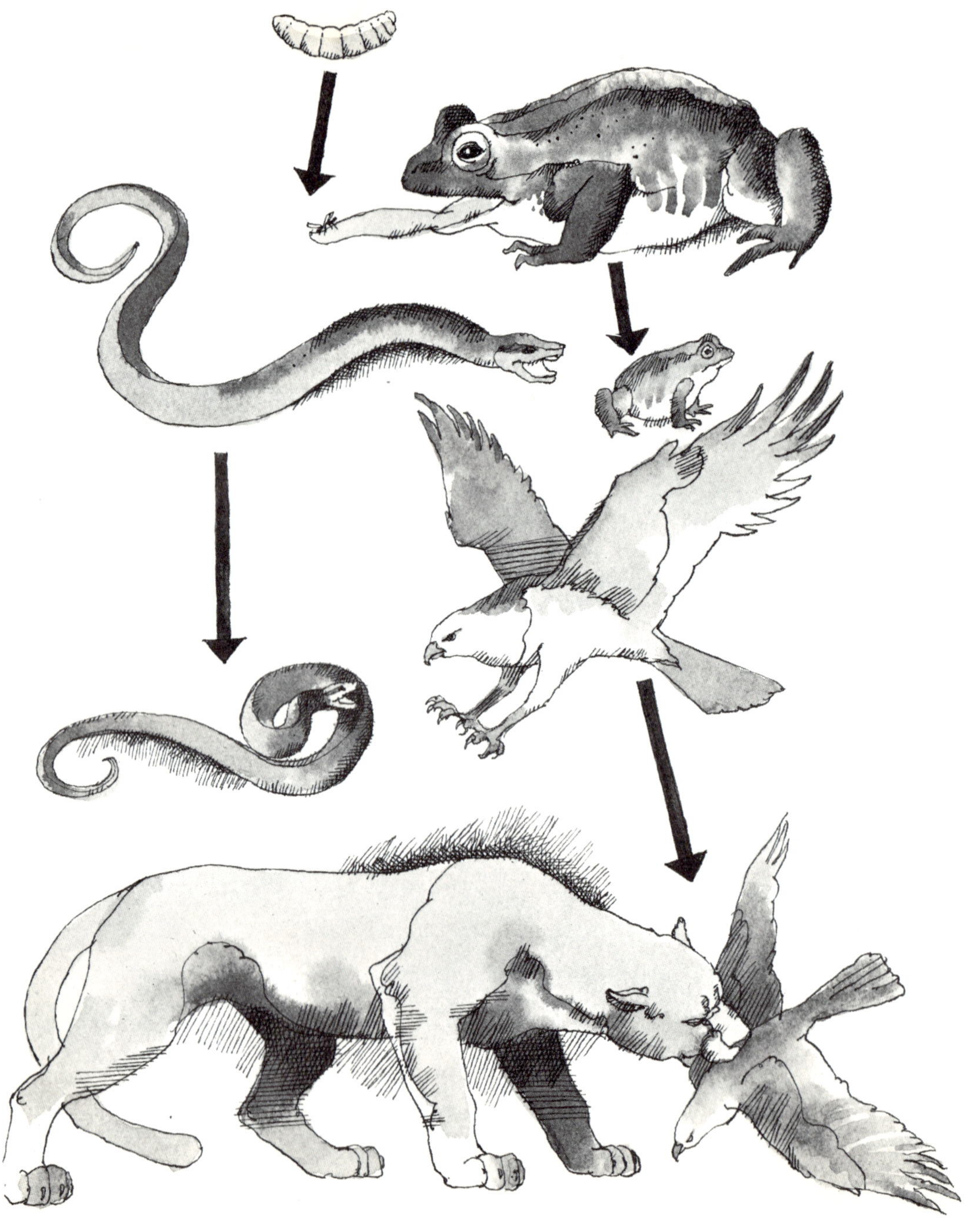

consume the milk of some forms of cattle. Since we also eat considerable plant life, we are called *omnivores*. A cat or dog will sometimes chew upon or consume grasses and other plants, but since its main diet is meat, it is classed as a predator, not an omnivore.

Another food chain example begins with an insect larva, which feeds upon microscopic plant life. It eventually becomes an insect that is eaten perhaps by a frog. The frog may then be caught by a snake, which is then snatched up by a bird — which may be caught by a larger bird, such as a hawk. The hawk may then be caught by a mountain lion. And so it goes: All life has its place somewhere in a food chain, within the environmental ecosystem where it dwells.

The food chain process is regarded in three basic ways. The most fundamental chain — from plant life to the last predator in line — is called the *predator chain*. Each successor in the chain is physically larger than its prey. In the *parasite chain*, a plant or animal derives its energy or shelter from a larger life-form. The lice and other parasites in or on a bird are examples of this form. The process is of course exhausting to the usually unwilling "host," and if the parasites consume too much from their host, it may perish. The third and last type of food chain is the *saprophite chain*. These life-forms derive their supply of the original solar energy from life that has perished. They are the decomposers that, by using dead matter as a source of energy, restore these materials to reusable forms. Fungi and other microorganisms are examples of these decomposers that are so important in the recycling of life in an ecosystem.

The Pyramid of Numbers

The food chain is a process of repetitive food consumption —
all of which begins with solar energy. With each such consumption, an energy transfer takes place which involves
losses. For example, those animals that are warm-blooded use
some of the food energy they consume to maintain their body
heat. Because of these losses at each stage of the food chain,
the mass amount of life the consumed food will sustain is reduced. It takes much sunlight to grow a plant. In terms of the
raw energy of the sunlight that falls on the plant, only a portion of it — little over one percent — is actually used to grow
the plant.

When the plant is eaten — and it takes a large amount to
feed a herbivore like a cow — the energy used to heat the cow
is not retained, and so this energy is lost. When the cow is in
turn consumed, not all of it — the bones, hide, and so forth —
is eaten, and so the part of the original energy that produced
the bones and hide of the animal is not passed on along the
food chain. In short, with each use of the energy in the food
chain, more and more of it is lost along the way, and it becomes an increasingly inefficient process. Therefore, the bulk
numbers and sheer mass of living material at each successive
food chain stage decrease.

Put another way, the mass bulk and numbers of earth's
green vegetation are the greatest among all life-forms. The
life-forms at the other end of the chain, such as man, huge

cats, and so forth, are numerically fewer and of less mass. The pyramid represents this pattern. If man is the last in the chain, and atop the pyramid, the life he fed upon is greater in numbers and mass than himself. That life which supported what man consumed is even greater in numbers and bulk. Were you to trace the individual life-forms a given man consumed right back to the first plants consumed — through all the steps in between in the food chain — the total mass and numbers of life involved would be tremendous.

The Checks and Balances
That Preserve Harmony in an Ecosystem

Every ecosystem has what is known as a *carrying capacity*. Like seats on a train, there is room for comfortably carrying only so much passenger traffic. In an ecosystem its seating capacity is the number of *"niches"* it has to offer each individual species of life that lives in the ecosystem. Just how many of these niches there are — places in the environment — depends upon how much and how adequate are all the available environmental physical factors that are important to the various life-forms that inhabit the ecosystem. These factors include the water, air, temperature range, physical places of seclusion and protection, shape, or openness. All totaled together, these factors determine the ecosystem's carrying capacity. If there is too much of one factor — a particular life-form in too many numbers, or too much water due to a flood — there become too few niches to support all the life in the ecosystem, and the "balance of nature" in it is upset.

Each species of life in an ecosystem has the ability to reproduce itself at the rate it can produce young, eggs, shoots, spores, runners, or whatever its particular means of reproduction. This theoretical ability on each species' part to reproduce its kind is known as its *biotic potential*. In reality, only a small portion of each species' progeny actually survives, and many individuals, being a part of the food chain, are preyed upon — or they perish in one way or another. And so the numbers of a species are a result of the biotic potential restrained by environmental pressures. The availability of the niche each species occupies in the ecosystem plays an important role in keeping a harmonious balance within the system.

But even so, there is constant change in an ecosystem as each life-form reproduces itself, consumes, or is consumed — or perishes and is reduced to its raw origins by the decomposer life-forms. The food chain cycle, with all its intricate variations, contributes much to the basic stability and balance of a healthy ecosystem. And the larger and more complex the system, the better able it is to keep itself in balance, for the more forms of life there are in an ecosystem, the more restraints there are that keep any one form of life from dominating. An out-of-balance condition can come about when there is too much of one form of life, or if one form should chance to vanish.

How Life-Forms in an Ecosystem Influence and Control Others

Where there is an abundance of a certain life-form, whatever life-form feeds upon it finds the going easy. With plenty to eat, it grows in healthy profusion, and reproduces its kind at a faster rate. Should it chance to overproduce its kind, and become too plentiful, there will be less food to go around for that species. Each of the species will of course then increase its efforts to find the now-scarce food, and in doing so will deplete further the life-form upon which it preys. With there being so little of the preyed-upon and once-plentiful food on hand, the predator finds the going very much harder. In the search for food some members of the species will starve, and in their quest for food, some may become so preoccupied as to become less wary — and make it easier for *their* predators to capture and consume them. Actual lack of space can also be a limiting factor. In time, under these poor conditions, the species is reduced in numbers. The life-form on which it preyed now finds itself under less pressure — and so begins its own comeback process. (What *it* preyed upon has had a long period of grace, and may now be quite plentiful.)

This process can ripple back and forth through the food chain. The now-reduced life-form had a predator as well, and it may now have become the overpopulated life-form and the one beginning to feel the pinch for want of its depleted food. The species will now begin to shrink in numbers by the same process.

The ebb and flow in the numbers of each species can be markedly cyclical in nature — particularly if seasonal variations in the physical environment of the ecosystem are marked. Let us examine a cycle where marked climate change is involved:

In a temperate climate, a rabbit feeds upon vegetation. In the spring, those rabbits that have survived the winter begin to forage on the renewed source of food. Life becomes easier for them; the rabbits thrive upon the vegetation, and in turn reproduce healthy young rabbits in large numbers. Soon there are lots of rabbits, and so such predators as hawks and foxes find it easy to catch them — and these predators thrive. With the end of summer, the vegetation diminishes, and the rabbits are the first of this group to feel this seasonal change. Their predators still find the search for food easy, for the rabbits are busy foraging all the harder — and tend to expose themselves. But when their numbers are reduced by their predators, it is now the predators' turn to find the search difficult. And they, too, become pinched because of their own

overabundance; feeling the difficulty at the end of this seasonally influenced balanced-imbalanced cycle.

This temperate climate is one of extremes, for it is not confined simply to a constant shifting within the food chain. In temperate zones, the food chain process as a whole is almost completely arrested in the wintertime. In tropical areas there is not as much seasonal arrest of consumption by the life-forms in tropical ecosystems, although there is fluctuation between wet and dry seasons. The temperate zone example was given to introduce an important living activity that takes place in all ecosystems — but one that is more marked and more easily identified in temperate zone ecosystems. And that is the importance and ability of life-forms to *adapt* to their environment.

Adaptability — How Communities of Life Survive in an Ecosystem

The ability of each species of life to adapt to the physical conditions in its environment plays an important role in how it fits into the biome of an ecosystem. Those life-forms with a simple set of living activities tend to be less affected by variances that take place in their ecosystem. Each species' set of living activities is what enables it to thrive somewhere in an ecosystem.

The biome of an ecosystem may contain a great variety of life. On first sight it may seem hard to regard the life as other than a total grouping. Ecologists, however, regard the total

life-forms as being a number of communities of life. A "community" is made up of all the life-forms in a particular location that are directly bound together by important interrelationships — that are dependent upon each other for any of a number of reasons. Such a community of life-forms is known as a *biotic community*.

Regardless of the nature of each life-form's living activities — simple or complex — or in what biotic community it resides, its ability to adapt, and the nature of its adaptations, determine where in the biome of an ecosystem it will find its niche. Those life-forms with specialized or unique activities will thrive in their particular environmental niche. But at the same time such specialization can severely restrict that life-form. The woodpecker, for example, has developed a unique way of finding food under the bark of a tree. And by having developed this unique boring technique, which would be brain-jarring to almost any other animal, the woodpecker taps a source of food few other animals can get at, and so they cannot deprive him of it. But at the same time, the woodpecker can live only where he can find this unique food source. Were the woodpecker to fly into an area where the trees in which his food source exists are absent, he could not remain there for want of the food. And so his unique special activity is quite limiting to him. In large ecosystems, this may pose little problem, for his niche may exist almost anywhere in the system. His living activities include "staking out a claim," as it were — with noisy singing that serves to warn other woodpeckers of the same species that this or that area is "his" place, and

to stay away. Many songbirds exhibit this territorial-claiming behavior as one of their living activities; their "song" is often the expression of their claim.

The ways animals and plants adapt to their environment — a long-term process — are remarkably varied and sometimes very complex. The simpler their set of living activities, the less restrictive are their movements in and about their ecosystem, and their ability to tolerate extremes in the physical changes that take place in an environment. The animal that can eat almost anything — plant or animal — can move about more freely than the animal that eats only one kind of food. The condor and vulture are birds that eat carrion (dead flesh), and they are extremely mobile. While they, too, are limited to a set of physical factors — they cannot endure extreme cold, for example — they live in an ecosystem that is broad, and which bridges many smaller ecosystems. To the other extreme, the koala, a marsupial found in Australia, is an animal whose diet is largely limited to the leaves of the eucalyptus tree. The koala fares well in *his* ecosystem — but only where eucalyptus trees are present to provide his unique food. And so this particular special living activity severely limits the koala's choice of habitat. He cannot depart more than a meal's distance from his niche in the ecosystem.

In temperate zones, all the life-forms that exist there have to adapt to a seasonal variation of temperature extremes that markedly arrests food consumption by most of the life in that area. Remember the earlier example of the seasonal vegetation-rabbit-hawk food chain: It ended with the arrival of winter. Let us continue the example by including adaptability in the picture.

All the animals and plant life of that food chain have adapted themselves to this environment by developing ways to endure the winter period — when in most cases the food cycle is nearly arrested.

Plant-life production comes to virtually a complete halt during winter weather. But the plants have adapted to the situation by having produced seed able to endure freezing weather and which will germinate with the return of warm spring weather. Or the plant's roots will have stored enough food during the previous season to enable it to sprout new shoots when spring comes. With the new shoots and leaves the photosynthesis process starts again to produce the food vital to the plant and the life that in turn feeds upon it.

The rabbit, at winter's arrival, has prepared itself in several ways to bear the rigors of the cold season. It has grown strong and fat on the food which was plentiful in the summer. It will also have grown a thicker coat to shield its body from heat loss in the cold winter air. Some rabbits, with this preparation, may hole up somewhere — away from the extremes of surface cold — and sleep away much or all of the winter. This long sleep is called hibernation. During this time of sleep, the animal's life-support requirements are less. The sleeping animals draw upon their stored fat to keep them alive. Much of this energy is used to keep their body temperature at a fixed level, although sometimes at a lower level than it is in warm weather.

The snake, at winter's approach, has also developed a solid flesh that will provide for its food needs during the cold winter months. Being cold-blooded, it will not have to use any of the food energy to heat itself. As the days grow shorter and colder, the snake goes into a burrow where it can escape frost — temperatures below the freezing point of water — and sleeps out the winter.

The hawks, foxes, coyotes, large cats, and other animals like bears have adapted themselves in one way or another to endure the winter, with little or no food. All rely heavily on stored fat and a thick coat to provide them energy and shelter from the cold weather during the winter. Those that perhaps started out with too little fat, because they were ill or too crippled to get enough to eat during warm weather, may well perish during winter.

When spring returns, all emerge — usually much thinner than when winter began — to begin the cycle anew. The key to their being able to endure the extreme variation in tem-

perature in their ecosystem is their ability to adapt. Some animals migrate to warmer climates during the winter months. Scientists believe the cold temperature is one factor producing the migratory impulse. Many birds are among the animals that leave their summertime environment. Life in other more tropical ecosystems could not survive even one cycle of the temperature extremes in a temperate zone. They are not able to adapt to any break in their food chain cycle, and they may lack ways to survive the cold itself.

Ecosystems — Side by Side, or Within Each Other

We said earlier that a certain physical environment is not continuous, but is rather a series of "islands" wherein sets of physical factors combine to make an ecosystem-home for a biome of life. All the life in a given biome shares the ability to thrive in the particular set of physical conditions that exist in its ecosystem. There may be borders in the environment

where one biome ends and another begins. This abrupt contrast is seen where a major geological condition introduces a marked difference in the physical nature of the environment on either side. A mountainous topography right next to a flat plain can serve as the boundary between one ecosystem and another. The place where the continent ends at the seashore makes perhaps the most marked boundary of all. The lifeforms separated by a boundary are usually completely different from those on either side, for the physical factors that

exist on either side of the boundary are also completely different. Contrasted with the atmosphere of land is the water of the sea. While wind moves air across land, currents move water.

Even where ecosystems meet, however, there is not a sharp demarcation between the life of one ecosystem and that of the other. For instance, in the case of the seashore, the area between the high- and low-tide marks contains a wealth of life that lives there, and there alone. A region like this that separates one major ecosystem from another is called an *ecotone*.

A common boundary is the one between forest and grasslands, or savanna. Seldom does a clear, straight-line border mark where tall trees stop, but it is often sharp enough so that one may be able to walk from the forest out into the open in a matter of several minutes. Sometimes there is little obvious difference in the land to explain why this area has become the boundary between two large ecosystems. But the differences exist, and the life-forms that reside on each side of the border, and *in* it — the ecotone — often play their own part in keeping the border intact.

Much of the plant life that lives in one ecosystem could also live in the bordering ecosystem, except for the presence of the other ecosystem's vegetation, and certain members of its animal life. For example, grass and other low-level shrubs and related vegetation must have their share of direct sunlight to thrive. If seeds of grass are blown or carried into the forest side of a border, the grass may well germinate and grow for awhile on the stored seed energy, but the taller trees will shade the ground so that the grass cannot obtain enough light to mature so it will waste away.

The trees, on the other hand, may drop seeds just over the border in the grassland side which will germinate and grow. Were they to survive to be tall trees, they would push back the grassland by the amount of shading they produce. But such "invaders" may well be kept out by the life-forms in the grasslands. The established life-forms may be seed-eaters, or animals that feed on shoots. The controls vary in many ways and may be quite unexpected. A tree might survive several years and be well on its way to becoming established, when a sheep or other grasslands creature might chew the bark off its stalk — or tear it apart while rubbing its horns on it.

As long as the environmental conditions in each side-by-side ecosystem remain basically constant, the two systems and the blending ecotone between them will persist and remain relatively fixed.

When physical changes do occur in the environment, however, the life affected in many cases will adapt to the changes. Long-range physical alterations may require centuries — such as the coming and passing of an ice age — while others may come with a flash of lightning and a devastating fire. In both cases, as physical changes take place in an ecosystem, the life in it responds and adjusts by a process known as *ecological succession.*

The succession is an orderly process in which the life-forms that can adapt to the changes do so, while those that cannot adapt move elsewhere — or perish — and new patterns of community life take shape. If the physical change is permanent, a new biome makeup ultimately evolves, wherein the relationships between life in the ecosystem and its new physical factors become harmonious and constant.

In the case of an abrupt change — such as would come about by a fire burning a deciduous forest — the ecological succession that will take place afterward may well bring the

affected environment back to the state that existed before the fire, if given sufficient time. The basic physical nature of the ecosystem was only momentarily changed, and then the system returned to its normal state.

The fire will have destroyed much of the forest life — the dominant tree vegetation and the life that lived under its canopy. In time, the first growth to appear may be that of numerous annual plants, such as grasses and grains, wild flowers and the like, that can thrive now that sunlight reaches through to the "forest" floor. And with them will come the animal life they support. At this stage of the succession a meadow has been created.

The succession continues. Vines, small shrubs, and berry plants develop and offer shelter to seeds constantly blowing in from the surrounding stand of forest. Seedlings sprout and develop. Insects, birds, and small animals find shelter and food in the now-established thicket. The grasses — shaded from vital sunlight — slowly disappear. The seedlings grow into trees that coexist with the seedlings of slower-growing trees. As adults, the slow-growing trees will be very tall and will become the dominant members of the deciduous forest.

With each passing year, the trees grow taller and shade more and more of the area beneath them. The thicket vegetation, deprived of direct sunlight, gradually diminishes. The underbrush becomes less dense and provides niches for more and larger animals.

The process reaches its climax when the vegetation living in the area is receiving sufficient light, and all the life-forms can survive and reproduce. The ecological succession that has taken place was one of returning the area to the deciduous forest it was before the fire. The other life-forms that are adapted to these forest conditions will have also moved in to fill the niches created by the restored forest. With the biome now in continuous orderly balance, it is known as a *climax community*. The process of ecological succession is complete.

A House in Good Order

Life in any ecosystem should follow a basically harmonious existence. A healthy ecosystem is a house in good order. This sense of dynamic order throughout the whole ecosphere that surrounds the earth is called by many people *the balance of nature.*

In the past, it has been popular to think of existence in the natural environment as being savage and brutal. It was to many a dog-eat-dog, fiercely competitive situation, full of tyrant beasts preying on helpless ones. Man tended to regard the border between where he lived, and where the raw natural environment began, as the frontier. Where man lived, it was "civilized"; where nature began, it was the cruel and harsh "law of the jungle."

Life in the natural environment is in reality one of harmonious cooperative coexistence, where most life-forms are highly dependent upon each other. True, there are fangs and claws. There is occasional violence, for predators must eat, and to eat they must kill what they eat. And as a process of perpetuating the species there may be battles between the males of some species over the females. But the violence associated with these living activities is necessary and usually quickly done. Seldom is there any needless pain inflicted upon the prey, and conscious cruelty is not practiced by animals other than man. The lion and the hawk do not spend their time perpetually picking upon their prey. Once fed, they pursue other interests — caring for their young, sleeping, playing. As for the small amount of violence that is inevitably associated with the ecological food chains, it is a necessary part of the fundamental living process. In the overall view, the system is far and away marked more by cooperation or coexistence between living organisms than by outright conflict and competition.

Special Relationships Between Life-Forms

The cooperation that often takes place between living beings in an ecosystem can be remarkable — and sometimes quite advanced. Many species of animal life live together; indeed, some life-forms must do so if they are to survive at all.

The terms "herd" and "flock" apply to animals of one kind that group together for both companionship and mutual support and protection. In some cases, there is a social order that dominates the group. In the wild, bison, sheep, horses, and such predators as wolves will group together, and one of the males usually serves as their leader. Strength and stamina earn leadership, and there may be some battling between two would-be leaders. Seldom is one of the two killed in the process of settling the issue, but the loser may have to leave if he is defeated in a bid to assume or retain leadership.

Animals that live in groups graze or hunt together. In the case of wolves, which travel in packs, the members of the group share their food. Certain cattle such as bison, under attack, may form a circle, with their heads — and horns — faced outward, so that they can ward off an attacker from any direction.

Where flocks of birds are concerned, several of the birds may stay up in a tree where they can keep a sharp eye out for trouble, while the rest of the flock may be feeding on the ground. At the slightest alarm, the "sentinels" will cry out, alerting everyone.

Perhaps the most specialized and highly developed forms of group cooperation are found among insects that live in colonized communities, and that must do so in most cases to survive. Most noted among these are honeybees and ants. These insects have developed a way of life that requires that they live together to survive and reproduce. Within a given hive of bees, certain bees do special chores. And to be able to do these special chores they are physically different from others in the hive whose chores differ from theirs.

BEES: WORKER   QUEEN   DRONE

In each hive, there is a queen bee whose sole job is to produce enough eggs to reproduce the species. Depending upon whether the queen lays fertile or nonfertile eggs, and the use of special food for the young, they can become any one of the special bees in the group: drones (the only males in the hive), worker bees that build combs to store the honey they collect from flowering plants, and periodically a new queen who will depart the hive with some of the workers — to form a new hive somewhere else.

Many species of ants have similar living activities. One, the parasol ant, also engages in a unique form of underground agriculture. The worker ants bring small clippings of leaves into special underground burrows where they are used to grow a fungus upon which the ants feed.

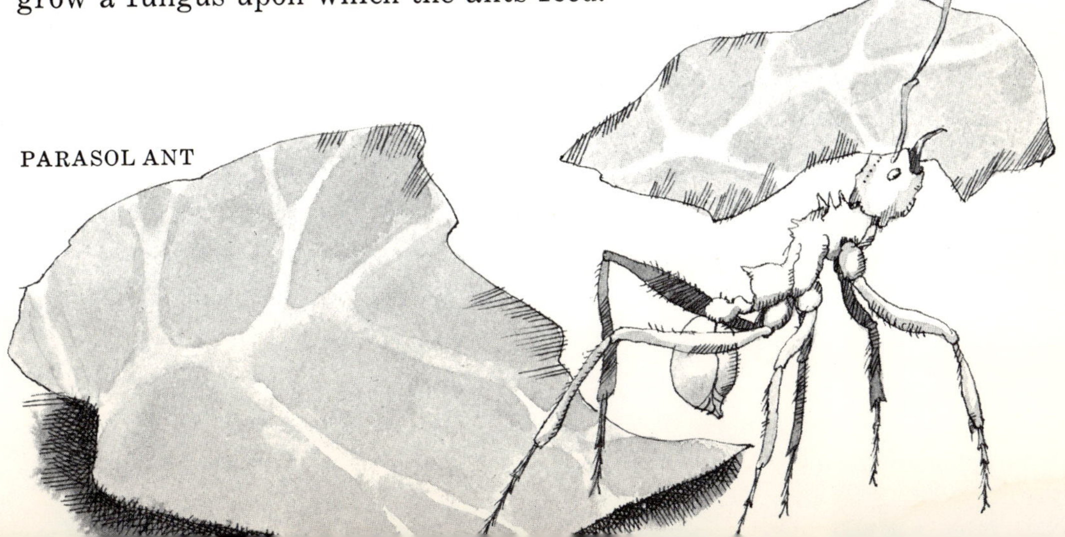

PARASOL ANT

Symbiosis

The combination of different species of animals or other life-forms living together is known as *symbiosis*. This process is not a food chain proposition, but a relationship in which the one animal or plant provides some benefit to the other. In a manner of speaking, it is a case of one animal finding his niche in the ecosystem, *in* the living activities of another animal.

Animals that live together symbiotically do so in two ways: Where they must do so to survive, their living-together activity is called *mutualism*. Where the relationship between them is not so binding — or where one simply benefits from the other, after the fashion of birds that thrive on the ticks and leavings of cattle — it is known as *commensalism*.

Symbiotic relationships can be very simple and direct — and sometimes startling. There is a bird that likes to pick bits of food matter from the teeth of a crocodile, while the latter makes no move to snap up the bird for a light lunch!

Man's relationship with milk-producing cattle is a fair example of commensalism. The cow suffers no loss by being milked. Actually, man has elevated this relationship into the two-way street that is more like mutualism in that man provides for the cow's needs in exchange for the milk. There is a similar example of this "agricultural" mutualism in nature. Certain kinds of ants act as "shepherds" to a cluster of aphids while they feed upon plant life. The aphids develop large quantities of a sugar liquid which the ants "milk" from the aphids. The ants shelter and care for the aphids in their underground nests, taking them out in the spring to where they can resume their parasitic feeding upon plant life — and their production of more sweet liquid for the ants.

Some forms of symbiosis can be more complicated, and two entirely different relationships can be associated in some important way. The three-toed sloth of South America is involved in one symbiotic relationship and also benefits from another one involving the cecropia tree.

The three-toed sloth grows considerable algae in its coat, which contributes much to its camouflage in jungle vegetation. (Staying out of trouble is almost the only defense for the three-toed sloth.) There is a small insect that lives in its coat and feasts on the algae. Found nowhere else, it is properly called the sloth moth. It does a good job keeping the algae growth down to proper proportions.

The cecropia tree found in the same jungle ecosystem grows tiny chambers into its stalk as it matures. An ant colony takes up permanent symbiotic residence in these built-in apartments. They are present in great numbers as anyone who has

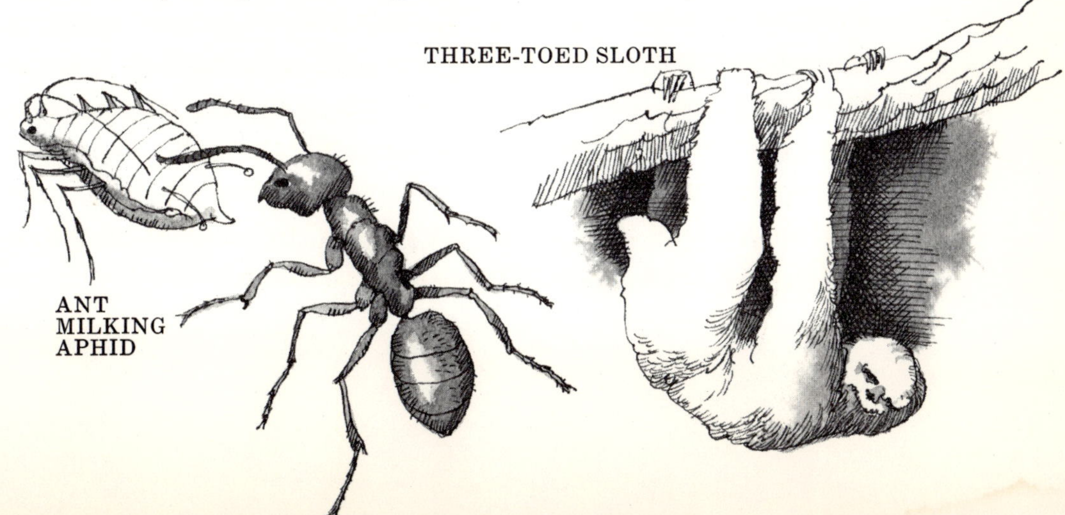

ever cut down one of these trees can tell you. One swing of a cutlass, and you are showered with cecropia ants.

The sloth is strictly a plant eater — and high on its diet are the leaves of the cecropia tree. In eating the leaves, the sloth cannot help but consume a few of the ants, for they are soon all over everything while the sloth is eating.

But these ants are quite important to the sloth, for they are rich in the particular trace elements that are vital to the diet of the sloth. Were it not for the symbiotic relationship that exists between the cecropia tree and the colony of cecropia ants that live in the built-in chambers grown by the tree, the plant-eating sloth would be deprived of the vital trace elements provided by the few ants he inadvertently consumes.

The symbiotic relationship of the cecropia tree and its ants is vital to the sloth's existence — whose existence of course is just as vital to the sloth moth that finds its niche only in the algae-filled coat of the sloth.

This example is but one set of symbiotic relationships that exist in varying degrees of complexity and interrelationship throughout the ecosphere. But it serves to show how infinitely varied are the living activities between the life-forms in the environment, and how delicate the balance between them can be under many circumstances. The balance is no less delicate in the ecosystems beneath the surfaces of the oceans — from whence all life is believed to have originated. Though water surrounds all life there, as does air, on land, the same ecological principles govern this life as well, with all its interrelated intricacies and symbiotic relationships.

Part Two

Man–the Reasoning Toolmaker

Man Changes the Land

Until quite recently man has regarded himself as being something quite above or outside of the "natural" environment — special among all life-forms and even ruler of the earth. From an ecological point of view, man remains another creature among many, with his niche in the environment — and just as dependent upon the mechanisms and stability of the earth as are other life-forms.

But it cannot be ignored that man *is* different in an important way. He reasons and plans and has developed these abilities so that he manages his life in ways no other creature can do. Chief among these is man's ability to devise, to make, and to use tools. This toolmaking skill may sound simple, but it was the extension of this ability that enabled man to set foot on the moon. It is at the root of every accomplishment that man has ever achieved.

Man's work began with simple weapons he fashioned to

hunt and fish and tools he designed to engage in farming. To serve his other needs, new tools followed. Columbus's boats were fashioned by tools and were themselves tools of transportation. With them he could travel long distances over water. By using tools, man devised ways to print books that assisted the spread of knowledge. Man's process of toolmaking has brought us every form of the transportation and communications tools we use today — from aircraft and space vehicles to television and computers.

The equipment man has devised marks an important difference between man and other life on earth. He is indeed different from all other life in this respect, yet man cannot escape being a creature among all others when it comes to his dependency upon the ecological mechanisms that sustain and perpetuate his species. Nevertheless, his unique ability has enabled man to have a profound effect upon the environment that sustains all life.

Early in time, man's numbers were few. He learned to use some of his first tools to change his nearby environment to serve his own needs, and so he was already doing what no other animal could do — altering the world around him in a lasting way that suited his requirements. His planning enabled him, with the help of a few tools, to herd and husband livestock. He also changed the land so that the plant life he consumed was easier to obtain by growing it in quantity in one place near at hand. And he initiated techniques to conquer or control many of the predators and pests that preyed upon him, his animals, and his crops.

Man now lives all over the world, in great numbers, and is so advanced in his reasoning and toolmaking abilities that he can now affect the environment in many great and permanent ways. Man's "difference" has proven to be a significant one.

In exercising his unique capabilities, man failed in one important way. He made changes in his environment without having first learned enough about *how* the environment functions, to enable him to make these changes *wisely*. The environmental troubles we are experiencing today are the direct result of these inexperienced actions made from a poor foundation of knowledge.

Man Reasons — But Not Always Well

Man, without his tools, is a frail creature. He can run fairly fast, but not for long; he lacks the armor of the turtle; and he has little by way of fur or hair to shield him from the weather. Since he has no fangs or claws he would be an easy prey for numerous predators, but for his ability to think and reason and make tools and weapons to defend himself.

Man has put his powerful abilities to work in many dramatic ways. While we have come to feel that the ways man has handled the environment have often been destructive and thoughtless, we must remember that he made these changes largely in times when the world seemed limitless.

Man need not feel too guilty for what has been done, for it has only been in relatively recent time that we have come to know that there is only just so much to the world. After all,

up until about the time of Columbus, most of the world was unexplored and thought to be a great flat place. That it might be finite was not given much attention, except to fear of falling off the edge of it! Then man's numbers were still few, and if he was not successful managing his life in one place, he simply moved on to new land. And by and large, the little that man did to the land — in clearing and tilling it — was not lasting.

Only when the world was known to be round did man first get an inkling of the whole of it. He could then explore and map it and know how much land there was. Even with the first suggestion that the world *was* finite, it was nonetheless very, very big, with lots of room for the very few who dared in those times to venture into its unsettled regions. Man's means of transportation were still horses, crude wagons, and small boats with little more than sheets to catch the wind.

But in time even the New World was settled and people

managed to establish parcels of land over which they had reasonable control and could till for the crops they needed. The land beyond the edge of their clearing was an endless wilderness. The point at which their land ended and the wilderness began, they called the frontier.

The Frontier — The Endless Lands Grow Smaller

With the establishment of the United States, the frontier became not so much a boundary, but rather a line that separated the area where man changed his environment from that where it remained virtually unchanged. There had long been Indian populations living beyond the frontier, but they were few in numbers compared to the size of the wilderness. The way of life of the Indians enabled them to live off the land, rather than radically change it as the newcomers did. They had a reverence for the land, which is reflected in the lore and legend of virtually all the Indian nations and tribes. While some Indians farmed land, they did little to shape the environment to suit any special needs. Rather they sought their niche in it in much the same fashion of other life in the natural environment.

The newcomers from the Old World, however, chose to change the environment in many gross ways. In large part, this was due to their accustomed way of life that included extensive agriculture and animal husbandry. And so the frontier was progressively moved back as increasing numbers of settlers in the new nation sought open space. They developed numerous techniques and equipment to change the land they occupied in ways that would support their lives.

In the United States, the frontier was an important influence for a good number of years. Everything beyond it seemed inexhaustible — and the people took what they needed from the land and forests as though these were endless. Wood was used for timbered dwellings, and as the demand increased, toolmaking ability rose to the occasion. Ways of felling and processing lumber were improved, and to move the lumber and a burgeoning amount of much other produce, the nation built roads up to and into the frontier, and better wagons to ride upon them.

The Industrial Movement

Once man had become well established in the New World he put tools to work in ways that went beyond simple agriculture and home-building. Now that man was enjoying new levels of wealth and interests, he sought new additions to living: better homes, machine-made clothes — and machines themselves. A new demand was to be made upon the natural environment. It now had to yield up great amounts of the things that came from underground: coal, iron, and a host of other ores that were needed to make the new machines and products eagerly sought by this increasingly advancing society. But since a frontier still existed, the land beyond was still considered endless by most people and they took all they wanted to supply their needs.

The Awakenings of Ecological Consciousness

Not all men were oblivious to what kind of an exchange was slowly taking place. A few managed to glimpse into the future and see a day of reckoning approaching. In Europe, where the frontier did not exist, cities had long since grown large and confining to those who lived in them. Muddy streets and dirty canals and waterways were a part of city living. Modern sanitation had yet to come. Since people warmed themselves by burning fires, smog was a problem in early times. Queen Elizabeth I ordered people in London not to burn coal while Parliament was in session, so that those deliberating the affairs of state would not be inconvenienced by the smoke.

While the New World knew few of these problems, there were people who did note the difference between what man had done to parts of the Old World and what had yet to happen in the New World. In a letter to an old friend in Europe, Simon Bolivar made this remarkable observation in 1824:

In that tired Old World of yours you have seen only the remains and the refuse of overprovident Mother Earth. There, she is bent with the weight of years, by infirmities and the pestilent breath of men; here, she is a maiden, immaculate, lovely, adorned by the very hand of the Creator. No, the profane touch of man has not yet withered her divine charms, her enchanting graces, her unspoiled virtues.

Bolivar made this comparison between a supposedly spoiled Old World environment and one as yet fresh. A few others, particularly in this country, felt that the land was already being damaged. As cities grew, people grumbled about the congestion and other ills of early city life. Late in the nine-

teenth century, the city of Boston was becoming crowded. In a spark of early wisdom, Boston's leaders conceived of a system of natural refuges and open parks that would be particularly available to those in congested areas of the city, who were "more and more shut out from the beauty and healing influence of nature and scenery . . . more and more shut up in their tenements and shops." In New York City, Central Park was another result of the movement to preserve green space in the cities.

The First Symptoms of Ecological Disorder Are Felt — The Frontier Ends

Up until the first transcontinental railroad was built, the frontier was felt to be a firm boundary between man's world and the natural environment — still primitive and limitless to most people. True, California and other western areas were rapidly being settled, but they were far to the other side of the frontier lands. The frontier remained enormous and inexhaustible in most minds.

The industrial revolution was now a moving force in America. Forests were leveled for timber. Minerals were extracted from the land without regard for the natural environment. The frontier virtually dissolved with the relatively sudden demand for oil and mineral ores in the lands beyond and behind the frontier.

Man Fills a Continent

Even when the last vestiges of the frontier had vanished, men still felt that all they were taking from the environment was inexhaustible — or at the very least, of little consequence if it were ultimately depleted.

Large areas of natural environment now existed only where man found little reason to intrude upon it; mostly in remote places. Almost everywhere else he razed whole forests of timber; mined; tilled land; and killed wildlife in a devastating manner.

In only a matter of years, he cut down a bison population in the millions to near extinction. The animals were killed for their hides, but more often for but a few parts of meat that were considered a delicacy.

His agriculture, while harmless in primitive times, was to grow to such proportions that basic changes gradually took place in the physical environment. Changes in the soil, coupled with a climatic vulnerability due to endless open space that was once partially forested, made western areas in the United States ripe for the creation of a dust bowl. In the thirties,

when a drought came, whole states were brought low by this ecological disaster.

Throughout the years, feeble voices were raised — mostly by isolated individuals who now saw the day of reckoning more clearly. But too few of these people got together to make their concern known to enough other people willing to halt the abuses. Those who did listen were not convinced, for all these cries of alarm were over resources too plentiful to worry about. True, the bison was now found mainly in zoos — with a small wild herd here and there — but what did it matter? There was a nation to build, and a continent to tame. Few people would give serious attention to arguments that they were harming the environment.

Well into the twentieth century, Americans continued drawing upon the natural environment, with the same belief that their forefathers had held, that it was inexhaustible. But since so little now remained, the results were disastrous — and taking place at a runaway pace.

And the time had at last come when man's changes to parts of the environment were permanent: The scars of the dust bowl will probably be with us forever; places where great forests once existed are now barren; strip-mining has caused equally ugly unhealing scars on the face of the land. Man's mark upon the land was felt in all parts of the world. Mainland China was once well forested. Today, wood is an expensive commodity there.

Efforts at Restitution — The Farmer Among the First

Farming is of course an ancient practice. But until very recently, ecological management of tilled land was seldom practiced. A farmer would grow what he wanted, year after year — not knowing that continually growing one crop on a piece of land would gradually deplete the soil of certain essential materials. In nature, all kinds of plants grow in a given place and have a balancing effect. Some remove materials and others replace them. The process working in both directions tends to balance out the mineral and material content of the land. While some farmers knew that animal manure helped plants grow, few farmers gave this technique much thought. In the past, when the land finally failed to yield more of the same crops, the farmer simply abandoned the land and moved elsewhere.

In recent years, with fewer new lands to move to, farmers have sought technical help so they might learn why their crops failed. In time, they came to know that with one-crop agriculture they must supplement this one-way-only unbalancing situation by providing for the material losses the land suffers. One technique involved rotating crops on a given piece of land — one year growing a crop that removes certain materials from the earth, another year growing a crop that would replenish some of these things. And they further fertilized the land with special preparations that would make up for any losses crop rotation failed to take care of. Naturally, the farmer sought rotation crops, both of which were valuable to him commercially.

The farmers' new approach to the problem was one of the earliest efforts to develop an ecological point of view — to learn more about the natural mechanisms with which they were dealing. One way or another, they had to provide substitute mechanisms for those nature normally provided when all kinds of plants grew in one place.

But the farmers only addressed a portion of the whole picture, and though they were to improve their agriculture vastly, growing great yields of food, other problems evolved that have now affected the larger environment, of which agriculture is but a small part. The fertilizers farmers used on the land, thought beneficial to crop growth, washed into creeks and rivers. To this was added chemical pesticides — a menace of recent times. These pesticides are, of course, useful to crop growth, but their effect on other life has posed serious problems. One pesticide in particular — DDT — lasts so long that it passes through the food chains to animals we eat and has added to the water pollution problems already posed by the fertilizers. The use of DDT is now being subjected to government control.

And so, even though the farmers were beginning to become conscious of the ecological problems related to their farming needs, the solutions they came up with added yet new problems to the whole environmental picture.

As we moved into the latter half of this century, the earth environment was on a downhill road to serious trouble — all because the toolmaking animal did not use his tools wisely. And yet, as late as it was, it was still a matter to which only a relatively few people were devoting much attention.

True, a host of United States government agencies had long since been created to deal with this or that part of the natural environment. The Interior Department was given broad general management authority in environmental matters. Special and unique pieces of natural environment were set aside as national parks, to be kept as intact as possible. Certain wildlife was being protected on special refuges. Matters concerning many of the minerals, oil, and ores taken from the environment were watched over by this department. A Department of Agriculture was created to help make farming a better organized and more productive proposition. The Forest Service was created to deal with similar matters as they related to the extraction of timber and handling of public forests.

These agencies in many cases did indeed bring important ecological wisdom to the environment-managing affairs of the country, but most of them shared one flaw. Their approach to the natural environment was based mostly on how to care for it so it would yield as much as possible. The idea that the environment should be cared for because it is valuable — just as it stands — was understood by very few people. The nation had yet to know and appreciate the life-fulfilling role the natural environment plays in men's lives.

Man Builds a Sloppy Nest

At midpoint in the twentieth century there were still too few people who were concerned about what was happening to the environment to make their voices heard. Now we see one or another environmental problem on the front page of newspapers almost every day. This was not true twenty years ago. Though we were witlessly spoiling the remaining natural environment, the subject was seldom discussed in public print. And though we were then beginning to spoil our own man-made environment in ways most of us could now feel, even this caused little more than grumbling among a limited number of individuals.

Perhaps the finest of man's material accomplishments was his creation of cities. Over a long period of time, man had developed almost complete mastery over the elements. By the twentieth century, wheels — and roads — could take people anywhere, quickly. We could heat our homes and offices in winter and cool them in the summer. Man-made recreation — television, movies, theater — at its best in the city added further attraction. So more and more people moved into the growing cities. Today, three-quarters of all the people in the United States live in or around cities, and the major mass of commercial fuels, produce, and products follows them there.

With all these people now living and working in one relatively confined place, a host of new problems have beset the environment.

To heat — and cool — all the homes and offices in large cities, it takes great quantities of fuel. Much of it is burned right in or near the cities. A great many people also own automobiles and ride buses and use other kinds of vehicles which also burn fuels. All this fuel consumption pours gases and unburned wastes into the atmosphere over our cities. When there is no wind to carry these fumes away, they can hang over a city like a smoke screen. Sometimes the shape of the nearby land contributes to holding these fumes in place. Since many of the waste products of all our burning are poisonous or very noxious to the eyes and lungs, the situation can be very serious. In both Los Angeles and New York City, there have been times when people have died because the air became so polluted by fumes.

The problem began gradually, but with our steadily increasing use of these fuels, it has become so serious a health threat that all kinds of techniques are now being tried to prevent these wastes from getting into the air. Unfortunately, we still have to burn fuels to serve our city life and traveling needs, and few of the techniques we have tried so far have proven entirely satisfactory: The amount of fuels we burn continues to rise, and the air pollution problem is getting worse.

In the United States, the consumption of foods, products, and clothes has reached a high level. All the materials these products are wrapped in are creating a waste disposal problem in the cities. Today, we each throw away as waste material more than the bulk of the actual products our forefathers *bought* and used in years gone by. Potatoes came in a bushel basket, then, which was still doing hard duty around the farm, long after the potatoes in it had been consumed!

Just getting rid of all of today's trash in a modern city requires an army of workers using huge fleets of trucks to carry it away each day. And the problem of where to put it is greatest of all.

Only a half century ago, this posed little problem. There were always fields and open places, just at the edge of town. Today, such open places to dump our refuse are hard to find nearby — and yet we have much more trash to get rid of today than yesterday. In some areas the only place to dump our garbage is in the ocean, or in lands we wish to fill — on which to build more city, in which to house more people, who will throw away even more trash!

And the sanitary waste disposal situation has become just as serious. In smaller communities, for years the people used outhouses and septic tanks to put this waste in the ground. When sewer lines became practical — particularly in cities — raw sewage was often piped into nearby lakes or rivers which, in theory, would carry it out to sea. Where the amounts were small, there appeared to be little more than local difficulties because of the bad-smelling water. In time, modern sewage-treatment plants were created to minimize this problem, but sewage plants are expensive and take a fair amount of land — something that gets more and more scarce as cities grow and expand. Sewage treatment facilities have seldom been able to keep up with this constant expansion. And so sewage that could not be processed was simply dumped raw into our waterways. Today, many of our lakes and great rivers — once clear and clean-running — are now so polluted, people cannot swim in them, much less drink their waters. And this of course poses yet another problem: where to find enough clean water to serve the constantly growing fresh-water needs.

Industry that manufactures today's products and power has added to this pollution burden by dumping its chemical effluent into these same rivers and lakes. The result of all these abuses is that most of our natural waterways are now polluted. Their waters are unsafe to drink or to swim in, and some are so badly polluted that little or none of their original host of natural life lives in them anymore. Even some of our Great Lakes are becoming barren places of virtually lifeless

water. Of all the world's man-caused environmental problems, none appears so immediately dangerous as the destruction of our sources of clean water.

Where man has gathered together to live in crowded cities, the concentration of trash and wastes he produces is gradually making his cities unlivable. In some places, city dwellers live in a squalor of strewn trash and filth that was unknown even in the crowded cities of the Middle Ages.

But perhaps worst of all, in building his cities, man used the same technique he did in settling the frontier. He eliminated virtually all of the natural environment to make room for new buildings and roads. In this twentieth-century extreme of frontierism, he has surrounded himself with his own man-made concrete and steel environment. Little open space is left to relieve the monotony of the surroundings. While a few parks and corner greens may exist, even these oases of natural environment cannot always survive under the now ever-present blanket of man's airborne wastes.

The Effect Spreads

Although much of man's pollution originates in the cities, the winds and rivers carry it out to the surrounding areas. So much air pollution now exists it cannot be dispersed by the clean air outside cities. And cities are now found everywhere,

sometimes blending into each other, each adding its share to the sum total. The smog in the air sometimes extends for thousands of miles. Airline pilots who once flew into most cities through clean air now find the smog as much a navigational problem as naturally clouded or fogged climate.

The thoroughly polluted waterways of much of the country carry their filth out to sea. We once thought the ocean was too big to be affected — just as we used to feel the natural environment was endless and inexhaustible behind the frontier — but now we know better. We find remains of our pesticides in faraway arctic birds! Even the sea is not big enough to contain and dispose of our wastes. So at long last the question of where *else* to look for waste-disposal space receives an abrupt answer: There *is* no remaining place.

We Begin to Feel Responsible — and to Take Stock

When people begin to gasp and choke in their usual surroundings, they know they have a serious problem that demands a solution. In 1966, a peculiar atmospheric condition known as inversion occurred over New York City. Warm air covered cooler air over the city and remained static for several days. The static city air became polluted and more than a hundred people died as a result. Other cities had shared similar fates.

Los Angeles is situated in a bowl-like recess in the land, so that similar inversion layers affect it frequently. Cities abroad began to share air-pollution problems in the sixties. When large numbers of people perish from such causes it becomes news to more than concerned biologists, health specialists, and ecologists. The causes of the problem were exposed, and almost everyone wanted corrective changes made immediately. Overnight, air pollution became a major political issue.

But it was learned that changes would be no easy matter. People learned that *they* were the ones causing the problem and that *they* were the ones who would have to stop creating pollution in many, many cases. The questions were: Were they willing or able to stop driving their cars? To turn off the heat in their homes? To stop throwing out trash and garbage that had to be burned? To take no more airplane trips, or to live without foods brought to markets in trucks? A solution would not be simple. The causes of air pollution took years to develop, and they are closely tied to the fundamental processes that support almost everything we do to work and live.

Ecologically speaking, it is man's living activities that are now giving us trouble. Over the years, we have developed a new set of living activities that have long since replaced many of the more natural ones of our ancestors — living activities stemming almost entirely from our centuries-long toolmaking process. Many of our tools have now become a basic part of our lives — and are vital to us. We depend heavily upon the family car to handle our daily occupational needs, as well as jet aircraft and other vehicles to carry us and our products to distant places. Our new living activities in our home environment cannot take place without the fuels needed to heat and to cool it. Few of us grow our own food, and so it must be brought in to our cities by train and truck. And to handle and safely ship all these products and produce, we wrap them in great amounts of paper, wood, plastic, metal, and glass. All of these materials must be disposed of somewhere, when we have consumed their contents.

The list of our living activities that are tied to the tools we have created goes on and on. We have now come to know that the shaping of our lives around and in a man-made environment has brought us grave trouble. It will be hard to undo completely the damage we have done, and are continuing to do to the environment, without upsetting our basic way of life.

We Stop What Can Be Stopped

Our first course has been to try to improve, however we can, the ways our tools are used — particularly those that are direct causes of pollution. The motor car has been found to be one of the major causes of air pollution. Air pollution was so bad in parts of California — Los Angeles, in particular — that laws were passed to compel the makers and users of automobiles to cut down their emission of air-polluting fumes and other wastes. Special devices now have to be used on new automobiles to make sure fuel is burned properly.

Open fires on dumps and use of incinerators have been stopped altogether in many places where these were found to be large contributors to air pollution. Industry and power-generating plants have tried changing to the use of fuels that emit less pollutants — and special devices have been installed in smokestacks to trap certain materials that earlier were released directly into the atmosphere. Jet aircraft engines are being redesigned all the time to make them burn their fuels in less polluting ways. All these and many other techniques have been tried to arrest somehow the causes of air pollution, while not depriving us of the machinery that has become vital to our way of life.

The same interest is developing in the control of water pollution. Industry has begun to make an effort to convert some of its waste products into forms that will not pollute the waters into which they flow, or else to find a place on land to dispose of these wastes. Sewage plant construction has been increased, and garbage and trash instead of being burned are dumped into areas needing landfill, away from waterways. But these developments have been very costly, and in many cases just not efficient enough. Air and water pollution continues to get worse.

As though things were not bad enough already, we have found that man-made materials are causing unexpected trouble. In the past, much of what we manufactured came from the natural environment and could be disposed of by natural forces — by rusting or oxidizing, rotting, slow combustion, and other processes. But in our search for newer and more durable materials, we put our knowledge and toolmaking abilities to work creating entirely new substances, ones never found in nature in the forms we created. They are often materials which cannot be reduced naturally, such as aluminum and many of the new plastics. When we dispose of them, none of the natural processes break them down, and so an aluminum beverage can will lie where it is thrown along some roadway — virtually forever. Only by burning many of the new plastics that bottles are now made of can they be reduced, and they are hard to burn in nonpolluting ways.

Perhaps the most ominous of the new, nonnatural materials are some of the pesticides we use on our crops and yard plants. Not only is nature unable to reduce them, they are also poisonous to many forms of life. DDT is just such a material that remains intact and poisonous for many years, no matter where the winds and waters of the world carry it. Aside from its being found in arctic birds, more close to home it collects in the organs of some of the animal foods we eat; the milk of cattle; and even in the milk of human mothers. It has sometimes been found in such concentrations there that babies could not drink their mother's milk safely! Although DDT is important to agriculture, its subsequent damage has been so great that its use has been discontinued in many places.

In our first efforts to do something about pollution's causes, we tried to "have our cake and eat it too" — by attempting to correct the pollution caused by our materials and processes, without having to do away with them. But pollution continues to get worse!

We May Have to Change
Our Living Activities — to Survive

With all the conscientious efforts to clean up our mechanical processes so they could still be used without further hurting us and the environment, no single effort has really worked at a price we can afford. And in the end we are still faced with the need to stop all pollution, if we are to arrest the ecological decline that is steadily taking place in the earth environment. More and more it is evident that to arrest this decline, we are going to have to sacrifice those of our tools and their uses that cause environmental problems, in favor of substitute tools. And if substitutes are not to be found, we may have to bear the change that will take place in our living activities if we find we have to do without them altogether.

In some cases, substitutes *can* be found. The automobile is one of our most important tools, and so we are trying very hard either to clean up the internal-combustion engine that runs it, or to find some other way to power the car so that it will not pollute the air. Steam and electricity are both receiving much attention as alternate ways to power motor vehicles, because they would produce little or no pollutants from the fuels they depend upon. While a battery-powered electric car would charge on power-plant-generated current and create a vast need for new generation facilities, the power plant use of the fuel is much more efficient than the way fuel is used in a vehicle engine. The overall pollutants produced would be

much less if fleets of electric vehicles were powered by central power plants.

We must heat and cool our homes, and so better power generation techniques will have to be developed (particularly if we are also going to run electric vehicles from the same source). Nuclear energy offers some promise for the future, since the plants using it do not burn fuels. The nuclear plants now being tried out may introduce their own new forms of pollution, however. They are water-cooled, and the heated water that is returned to rivers, bays, and streams may add thermal pollution to the growing list of ecological problems — unless imaginative ways to use this wasted heat can make it a useful product rather than a pollutant. Also, the risk of radioactive pollution is always present should the plants fail in the proper treatment of their materials.

We may not have to sacrifice all the troublemaking machinery and processes we depend upon, but in each case where we may have to do without them, the decision to do so will affect our way of life — our living activities will be changed by that much.

These problems are unique to man and most pressing for us today. In the past, we could move when things did not suit us where we lived. And when something attacked us as fiercely as pollution is attacking us today, it was usually an enemy we might fight and defeat in battle. For the first time in man's existence, he is up against an enemy he can neither flee from, nor conquer — for it is man himself.

A Hard Look at Man's Beliefs, About His Role in the Environment

Naturally man is not going to engage in battle with himself. But since a real conflict now exists between man and his tools and his future in the earth environment, the situation is just as serious as if a real enemy of the more time-honored kind were at his doorstep.

Man himself must alter his own beliefs and values, for it is these that have led him through time to this sad turning. Man's beliefs are of course very complex, and they differ in many social, cultural, and religious aspects around the world. At first, we can only single out those few beliefs that have obviously contributed the most to bringing man into conflict with the environment, and seek wherever possible to bring his beliefs more in line with environmental reality.

Perhaps greatest among these is man's historical belief that he is something apart from the environment — and its master. Many aspects of culture and religion have led men to think along this line. But regardless of the faith we have shared in this belief, we know that what has happened does not support it, and that we will not survive if we do not view our position in the environment in a more accurate way. We now know that we must change our ways of dealing with the environment to ones that reflect the needs of the whole environment — and not just our own.

This adjustment will call for a fundamental change in the understanding and beliefs of all men. Difficult as this kind of change may appear to be, it has happened before.

Before Copernicus and Galileo, it was commonly felt that the earth was the center of the universe, and that the entire universe revolved around it. This belief led men to come up with all kinds of strange theories to justify it — from odd mathematical formulas to visions of a hemispherical world, supported on the backs of giant elephants and turtles.

In time, a few wiser men realized the formulas did not make sense and so they suggested that maybe the earth was *not* the center of the universe but was rather just one of many planets in a solar system which was itself but a tiny part of the universe. They got in serious trouble, at first, for their

views were considered very upsetting to many fundamental
and long-standing cultural and religious beliefs. Columbus
was only one among many who had a hard time trying to
convince people he would not sail off the edge of the earth, in
his planned voyages into the uncharted seas to the west —
and he had great trouble getting financial support for his
expedition.

But as time passed, true knowledge about the universe
became known by more people and dispelled the notion that
the earth was the center of the universe. But in those days,
such knowledge was slow in developing, and so this old notion
persisted for centuries.

The idea that man is the center of life is a similar and
equally primitive concept and just as unfounded as the pre-
Galilean belief that the earth was the center of the universe.
It is this long-standing belief that has led us to treat the environment as we have and brought us to the troubled situation
we now face.

Fortunately, very much more is now known about the world
around us, and knowledge is more quickly spread today. The
concept that ours is a "man-centered" environment is fading
in the minds of most people in the face of gathering evidence
to the contrary.

And so it came to pass that the qualities that make man different from other living creatures — his ability to reason and
to make and use tools — are what got him into trouble with
the environment. His belief that he was so much superior to
other life led him to change the environment in any way he

chose, to suit his own needs on the grounds that they were more important than any other considerations. He built and used his tools to accomplish these ends — and so many of today's environmental ills. It is sad that man's uniqueness has been such a liability in this respect.

Restoring the Natural Environment

If man is to put his capabilities to constructive use, undoing the damage already done comes first. Our survival depends on radical repair work. No one is exactly sure just what will occur if our environment continues to degenerate at its present rate, but nobody's predictions are attractive. Changing values will take time, so some things will simply have to be done now in the simple faith that they are necessary.

  • We will have to try even harder than we have done so far to arrest pollution's causes. Our work has not done enough as yet — we must do more.

  • We will have to hasten every research effort to get us closer to the day we can replace every tool that harms the environment with one that will not.

  • We must acquaint everyone with the ecological problems we are facing — and that we must correct — so that when some of our ways of life have to be changed, people will know *why* and cooperate with efforts to correct our living activities.

Environmental Problem Solving

Knowing the *nature* of each environmental problem is most important. Solutions to environmental problems tend to fall into place somewhere between two extremes: *institutional solutions*, and *behavior-change solutions*. An institutional solution can take the form of a mechanical action that will correct a problem. A behavior-change solution requires a new set of actions from people.

An example of an institutional solution is the construction of a new sewer system — a process involving only a technical treatment by an institution such as government, coupled with the expenditure of the money needed to carry it out.

A good example of a behavior-change solution is solving a street and park litter situation. Just putting out trash receptacles as the necessary institutional part of the solution will not solve the problem. The actions of people are a necessary and vital part of the solution: They must be encouraged not to strew trash about, but rather to go to the extra trouble of putting the trash in a barrel. This calls for behavior change by people.

Naturally, institutional solutions seem the most predictably successful, but as far as environmental treatment is concerned, a great many of its needs today can only be attended to by people being encouraged to change their behavior in some manner.

(86)

Motivating Behavior Change

While people can be induced to do things for such reasons as patriotism, and a sense of overriding obligation, the most effective change results from a return that is personally felt, or rewarding in one way or another. These changes will not come easily, however, for man's present values took centuries to develop. And his behavior has been a reflection of these earlier values. We have come to know that many environmental problems call for man to change his behavior in many important ways.

Behavior change is hard to bring about without the proper motivation and necessary help and guidance. Knowing what kind of behavior change is called for is important. It usually takes place in one of two ways:

- People must stop doing something they've long been used to doing, or;

- They must do something they've never done before. Asking such things of people is hard, takes tact, and is a slow and patience-exacting process — a process best gone at right from the beginning.

Citizen involvement in bringing about environmental repair is one of the most effective tools in use today. Those groups that are the most effective have a firm grasp on the problem-solving process, and take care to answer three important needs when they seek to change people's behavior:

What must the people *know*, what must they *have*, and what must they *feel*?

People are reluctant to change their behavior until they thoroughly understand what's involved in carrying out a new routine — with full assurance that it will work. They will have to be provided any new equipment or services that are needed, to help them accomplish a new routine.

And perhaps most important of all, they must be motivated to carry out a new routine; to know why it's important, to *them*.

Bringing Elements of Natural Environment Back into Our Lives

Though we have long been working at the process of separating ourselves from the natural environment, there is much evidence today that we regret having done this so thoroughly. A great many people now pay money to enjoy what once was free. Visits to national parks, refuges, and wilderness areas occupy much of the leisure hours and vacationtime of Americans. Major efforts are now under way to secure more such areas and to restore others that have been damaged.

The yearning for some contact with the natural environment, which was once so plentiful, has become the basis of much of the turmoil we are witnessing today — particularly in our often drab cities, where the quality of life has become so inadequate.

We want to make our homes better places to live. More and more people have become dissatisfied with communities where houses all look alike and little or no natural "green" breaks the monotony. Most new community planning, reflecting these desires for natural environment near at hand, now includes open space as a vital part of the design.

We now look for ways to bring elements of natural environment back into our cities, and older communities, to offset their concrete and stone harshness. A back-to-nature movement is not what is called for, but rather a graceful blending of the natural environment with man's creativity. Parks and plentiful open space should become a part of all community-renewal efforts, and every vacant lot in our older cities should be given attention as a possible site for a bit of natural green in the heart of a city, rather than a site for yet another building. Concrete pools are good places to install a small sample of wetland ecology, instead of leaving them bare. Such designs would offer both quiet beauty and an opportunity to observe and learn about a phase of natural life.

To learn about the ecological mechanisms that govern life is to understand and appreciate them. And appreciation is what generates new values in men. A new sense of values will do much to make necessary behavior change an easier process.

We Must Add Ecological Understanding to Man's Knowledge Base

In the task of bringing the natural environment back into our lives, our schools have an essential role to play. It is just as important to learn about ecological mechanisms as it is to learn about physics and mathematics. Tomorrow's managers of the environment — both natural and man-made — are in school today. It is this group that must develop a more meaningful sense of values about the natural environment, and the vital role we now know it plays in the lives of men.

Since we have pushed natural environment so far away from where most men live — and learn — young people in United States cities are deprived of a feeling for the natural world and its processes. They are maturing with an unbalanced picture of nature, for the world of nature is not merely a beautiful legacy, but one that exhibits the basic formula by which all life on earth survives and perpetuates itself. By bringing elements of natural environment into the school surroundings and classroom — into the daily lives of young people, where they *are* — these processes can come to be a fundamental part of their fund of knowledge and give them the basis upon which to develop an environmental ethic that is constructive. With such an ethic and mature sense of values they will become reasoning toolmakers with the wisdom to do their reasoning and toolmaking *well.*

A New Sense of Values

To impart a knowledge about the mechanisms of the environment that can generate a permanent environmental ethic in the next generation will take years. To date, this subject has been sadly neglected at all levels of academic training. And to create such an ethic, a mature sense of values must develop out of the environmental learning process. Tomorrow's leaders must come to know intuitively, as man builds, that "this is good" and "this is bad." They will be able to make such judgments only when they have a mature sense of values to guide their judgment. In tomorrow's world, such judgment — backed by a new sense of values — will be vital, as man changes and manipulates the natural environment now left to us.

It is the learning process that will best bring about this ability to judge the good and the bad in our lives, and to generate the kind of values that will guide us:

• To buy cars that will not pollute the air — to sacrifice snappy high-powered performance, when it is not needed, in favor of fuels or vehicle power sources that will do an adequate job without fouling the air we all breathe.

• To be less wasteful in our use of water and other resources — so that sewage processing can be less of a problem and our clean-water sources will be under less demand.

• To change our consumption behavior so that we generate

less waste. Perhaps the day will come when each of us will pre-sort our trash — materials that are recoverable and those to be disposed of — into separate containers. In this way, glass and metals would be discarded in a manner in which they could be profitably recovered for useful purposes. These kinds of actions by informed individuals can not only reduce our trash volume, but perhaps make a useful product of some of it.

As time passes, the list of things we can do to change our living activities so that they no longer harm the environment will grow. But the key element in making these changes rests in the willingness of the public to change their behavior. The willingness to do so will come out of their knowing *why* they must change some ways of doing things, and what they will receive in return for the effort.

An Environmental Ethic for Tomorrow

"What's wrong with our environment" is a starting point to begin shaping a new ethic of nature. The problems that disturb people attract attention to our troubled environment. Oil-soaked beaches and seabirds, air no creature can breathe in comfort or safety, water that fish cannot live in, and the growing noise some of our machines produce — these are disturbing problems. What we do not like reaches into our own creation. We do not like our dirty cities; and more and more people now regret how cavalierly we pushed nature aside when we built those cities.

Through the learning process, tomorrow's citizens of the world will come to acquire values that can create a valid environmental ethic. The behavior-change process can then broaden from a purely personal reward base into one of a scope on the level of patriotism, family obligation, and social commitment.

As behavior change becomes increasingly easier — and effective — man's unique reasoning and toolmaking abilities can become the constructive skills they ought to be. He can then apply these abilities to the task of meaningfully redeeming and preserving the natural environment he has so badly abused in times gone by.

Bibliography

Carson, Rachel. *The Sea Around Us*. New York: Oxford University Press, Inc., 1961.

__________. *Silent Spring*. Boston: Houghton Mifflin Company, 1962; New York: Crest-Fawcett World Library (paperback), 1970.

Dubos, Rene. *So Human an Animal*. New York: Charles Scribner's Sons (also paperback), 1970.

Fuller, R. Buckminster. *Operating Manual for Spaceship Earth*. Carbondale, Ill.: Southern Illinois University Press, 1969; New York: Washington Square Press (paperback), 1970.

Gibbons, Euell. *Stalking the Good Life*. New York: David McKay Company, Inc., 1970.

__________. *Stalking the Wild Asparagus*. New York: David McKay Company, Inc., 1962 (also paperback, 1970).

Goldstein, Jerome. *Garbage As You Like It*. Emmaus, Pa.: Rodale Books, Inc., 1969.

Leopold, Aldo. *A Sand County Almanac*. New York: Oxford University Press, Inc., 1966; New York: Ballantine Books, Inc. (paperback), 1970.

Lorenz, Konrad. *King Solomon's Ring*. New York: Thomas Y. Crowell Company, 1952; New York: Apollo Editions (paperback), 1958.

Palmer, C. Mervin. *Algae in Water Supplies*. Washington, D.C.: U.S. Department of Health, Education and Welfare. Public Health Service #657, 1965.

Perry, John. *Our Polluted World*. New York: Franklin Watts, Inc., 1967.

Porter, Eliot. *In Wilderness Is the Preservation of the World*. New York: Ballantine Books, Inc. (paperback), 1969.

Soil Conservation Service. *Conquest of Land Through 7,000 Years*. Washington, D.C.: U.S. Government Printing Office. #A-1.75:99, 1953.

Storer, John H. *Man in the Web of Life*. New York: Signet-New American Library, Inc. (paperback), 1968.

Ward, Nathanial. *On the Growth of Plants in Closely Glazed Cases*. London: John Van Voorst, 1842.

Index